THE OUTDOOR PONY

by

Susan McBane

Illustrations by

Carole Vincer

KENILWORTH PRESS

First published in Great Britain by
The Kenilworth Press Limited,
Addington, Buckingham, MK18 2JR

© The Kenilworth Press Limited 1992
Reprinted 1994, 1996, 2004

British Library Cataloguing in Publication Data
A catalogue record for this book is available from the British Library.

ISBN 1-872082-30-0

Printed in Great Britain by Westway Offset

CONTENTS ■ ■ ■ ■ ■ ■ ■ ■ ■ ■

Introduction

Keeping a pony outdoors seems attractive in many ways. As a method of keeping, it may be cheaper (depending on whether or not you have to rent land) as savings can be made on food and bedding in some seasons. It is not as tying as the pony is not a prisoner in his stable waiting for his every need to be catered for but has freedom, food, water and company (or should have). The pony will probably be happier and healthier at grass, on the whole, *provided* he is well cared for.

But keeping a pony in a domestic field does not mean that he is living a truly natural life, although it *is* more natural than being stabled.

In natural conditions, ponies may have many square miles in which to wander, find their food and water and enjoy a natural herd life with plenty of companions and relatives of all ages and sexes. They are out in all weathers but may not suffer from exposure to the climate as they can find shelter in clumps of shrubbery, ranges of hills, cliffs or even hollows in the ground where they can get away from the wind, rain, sleet or hot sun. The domestic pony kept in a field rarely has access to natural shelter of this kind.

Animals evolve or develop to suit a particular area and climate – their environment – so wild ponies such as British native Welsh or Exmoors, for example, will be physically well able to live in their natural habitat and cope with the conditions. A domesticated pony has to live where we put him – but with suitable care you can help him cope with his less natural home and keep him healthy, happy and fit.

Different pony types

Your pony's type may be one of two extremes or he may come somewhere in between, as do most ponies. The pictures below show a typical native-type pony on the left, evolved by nature to live in the British Isles and places with a similar climate, and, on the right, a show-pony type containing Arab and Thoroughbred blood to give it the refinement and quality desired in show ponies today.

Britain's climate is mostly chilly and wet, sometimes quite cold with snow, ice and winds, so its native ponies have thick, long, almost woolly winter coats to help keep them warm and dry (next to the skin). In summer, when it is warmer, they have a short, sleek coat so they do not overheat easily.

They have chunky bodies with comparatively short legs; this body shape holds in heat. Also to retain heat, they have thick, long manes and tails, and the tails are held fairly low, so body heat is not easily lost from between the buttocks. Their nostrils are not as rounded (flared) as hotter-blooded ponies, again to keep in warm air, and their heads are bigger compared with their body size so cold air is warmed as it's breathed in. Their ears, which are thin and easily lose heat, are therefore small. Finally, their winter coats can resist rain and drain most of it away.

The ancestors of Arabs and their Thoroughbred relatives, evolved in hot, dry climates and so have opposite physical features – longer ears, thinner skin, smaller bodies, flaring nostrils, finer coats and higher tail carriages. They need help to live out in colder countries.

DARTMOOR

SHOW-PONY TYPE

Good and bad fields

A good field for ponies needs to have shelter, food (grass) and water. It should be well drained and slope gently to some outlet such as a pond or ditch (not necessarily in the field itself) so that the land does not become soggy in wet weather. It should not slope steeply, though, as ponies should have at least one flat area to rest on without having always to brace themselves against the slope, and sharp inclines can cause stumbles and falls.

Clay soils, which have very fine grains, are not good as they do not drain well. Their small grains hold water in winter, becoming sticky and heavy-going, yet bake hard together in summer and crack easily.

There must be a way of providing water for the ponies, either in a trough or other safe container (ponds and streams are often stagnant or polluted). Mains water piped to the field is ideal, or a tap within reach for a hosepipe.

Shelter is much more important than people realise. Look at the trees and any high hedges near the field: they will lean *away* from the prevailing wind. Therefore you need trees and thick hedges on the side of the field from which the wind blows, or a shelter opening away from the wind.

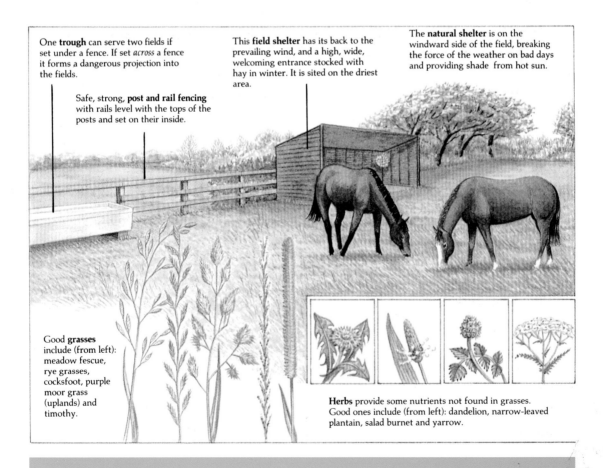

One **trough** can serve two fields if set under a fence. If set *across* a fence it forms a dangerous projection into the fields.

Safe, strong, **post and rail fencing** with rails level with the tops of the posts and set on their inside.

This **field shelter** has its back to the prevailing wind, and a high, wide, welcoming entrance stocked with hay in winter. It is sited on the driest area.

The **natural shelter** is on the windward side of the field, breaking the force of the weather on bad days and providing shade from hot sun.

Good **grasses** include (from left): meadow fescue, rye grasses, cocksfoot, purple moor grass (uplands) and timothy.

Herbs provide some nutrients not found in grasses. Good ones include (from left): dandelion, narrow-leaved plantain, salad burnet and yarrow.

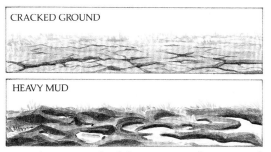

CRACKED GROUND

HEAVY MUD

Rich grass is bad for ponies; the type of poor-ish grazing used for sheep is better. Also, some grasses and plants are better for ponies than others; some may even be poisonous. Good and bad ones are shown in the pictures.

Fencing should ideally comprise strong wooden posts with firm wooden rails attached on the inside of the posts. If built thus, ponies cannot push them off when leaning over them (as they do), and they are less likely to injure their shoulders on the posts when cantering along the fence line.

Barbed-wire fencing is very dangerous but very common; ponies can badly tear their skin and legs on it. Ordinary (smooth) wire is reasonable if kept really taut. Wooden palings and chicken-wire netting are far too weak and metal railings can, again, be dangerous.

Wet, low-lying fields seethe with flies in summer and are waterlogged and unusable in winter; drier windswept ones offer no shelter.

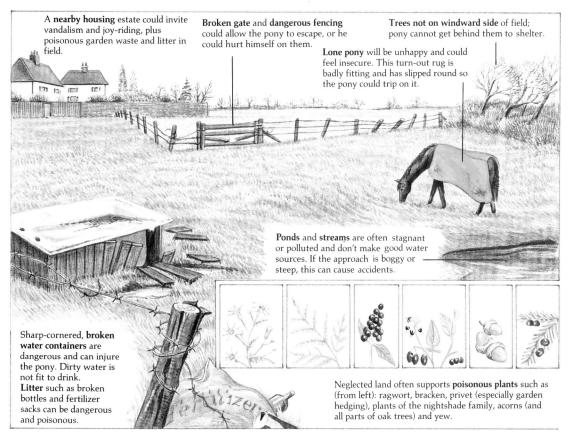

A **nearby housing** estate could invite vandalism and joy-riding, plus poisonous garden waste and litter in field.

Broken gate and **dangerous fencing** could allow the pony to escape, or he could hurt himself on them.

Trees not on windward side of field; pony cannot get behind them to shelter.

Lone pony will be unhappy and could feel insecure. This turn-out rug is badly fitting and has slipped round so the pony could trip on it.

Ponds and **streams** are often stagnant or polluted and don't make good water sources. If the approach is boggy or steep, this can cause accidents.

Sharp-cornered, **broken water containers** are dangerous and can injure the pony. Dirty water is not fit to drink.
Litter such as broken bottles and fertilizer sacks can be dangerous and poisonous.

Neglected land often supports **poisonous plants** such as (from left): ragwort, bracken, privet (especially garden hedging), plants of the nightshade family, acorns (and all parts of oak trees) and yew.

Skin and coat

Skin, hair and horn are 'related', being different versions of a similar material. They all need a correctly balanced diet to remain in good condition.

Skin is an elastic covering which protects the pony from the outside world. It contains nerve endings, so he can feel heat, cold, pressure and pain; it carries blood vessels; and it holds the hair roots. It produces natural oil (sebum) which makes skin and coat water-resistant, and it contains sweat glands. Sweat enables the pony to eliminate certain waste products, and the evaporation of sweat (which contains body heat) helps him to cool down when hot.

The coat creates, between its hairs, an insulating layer of warm air, helping to keep the pony warm in winter.

Ponies will stand with their tails to bad weather, so if living out need full tails to reduce heat loss from between their buttocks.

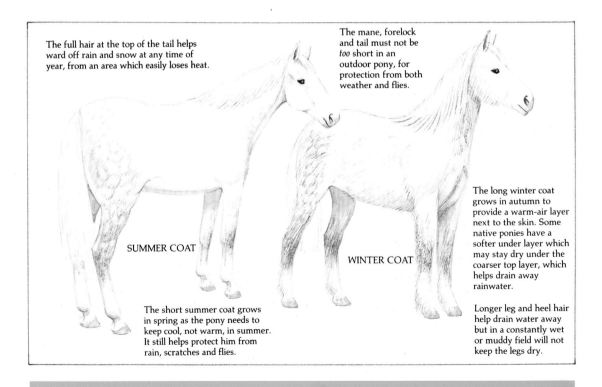

The full hair at the top of the tail helps ward off rain and snow at any time of year, from an area which easily loses heat.

The mane, forelock and tail must not be *too* short in an outdoor pony, for protection from both weather and flies.

SUMMER COAT

WINTER COAT

The long winter coat grows in autumn to provide a warm-air layer next to the skin. Some native ponies have a softer under layer which may stay dry under the coarser top layer, which helps drain away rainwater.

The short summer coat grows in spring as the pony needs to keep cool, not warm, in summer. It still helps protect him from rain, scratches and flies.

Longer leg and heel hair help drain water away but in a constantly wet or muddy field will not keep the legs dry.

The seasons

Spring – The main problem is over-rich grass which is very bad for ponies. There are no flies but the weather can still be cold and wet.

Summer – The problems now are hot, bright sun; constant torment from flies which can seriously inflame eyes; and hard ground which can lame ponies galloping away from flies.

Autumn – Fewer flies now, but grass produces a second spurt of growth which may cause laminitis, as in spring. The weather is usually mild and the pony starts growing his winter coat.

Winter – The ground may be very wet and muddy, even waterlogged, with no grass growing unless exceptionally mild. Ice and snow can ruin what grass there is. Ponies will almost certainly need extra feed. Remember to break the ice in troughs etc. twice daily when freezing.

Health and well-being

Although ponies are generally healthier and happier kept outdoors, this does not mean they are never ill, off-colour or unhappy. A careful eye must be kept on them, just as with a stabled pony. It is wrong to leave outdoor ponies for several days at a time without checking on them, as some people do. They should be checked twice daily as they could have an accident or become ill quite quickly.

Outdoor ponies are unlikely to suffer from COPD (Chronic Obstructive Pulmonary Disease) or 'broken wind', an allergic condition caused by stable dust and fungal spores on hay and straw, but may show hay fever-like symptoms during times of high pollen count. It is then best to bring them in away from the pollen, to a well-ventilated stable.

Laminitis, a serious foot disease caused by over-feeding, may occur on good grazing. Ponies need poor quality, but clean, grazing. If you can't arrange this, bring them in for part of the time or strip-graze their field with electric fencing, as for cattle. If you suspect laminitis, call the vet immediately.

Ponies don't mind cold, dry, still weather. Wind, rain, hot sun and flies can really cause suffering, as can very wet land which offers nowhere dry to lie and rest, which they prefer.

Worming is *very* important for outdoor ponies. Worms seriously damage ponies' blood vessels, stomach, gut and lungs and can kill them. You should worm ponies every six to eight weeks all year round, with drugs from your vet.

Healthy ponies are alert, feed well and associate with their friends. A sick pony will look miserable, may stay apart from others and be inactive.

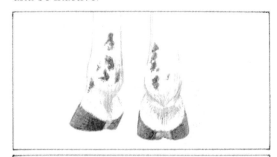

Mud fever (top) and rain rash or rain scald (bottom) are caused by the same germ. It attacks skin in wet conditions, causing pain, scabs and swelling.

Outdoor ponies can suffer from influenza and tetanus (lockjaw), so make sure that vaccinations are kept up to date.

Natural discharges should be sponged away from eyes and nostrils daily, as they can attract flies in summer and cause chapped skin in cold or windy weather. Dry the skin with an old towel after sponging. Remember that a nasal (nose) discharge can mean disease, especially if the pony seems unwell. If so, call the vet.

Remove 'bully' ponies from the field as they cause injury and stress to others.

Galloping on hard-baked ground in summer (usually clay) trying to get away from flies can cause chipped, split hooves, sore feet and jarred legs.

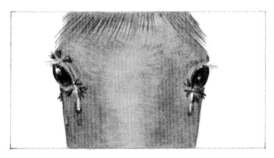

Flies really torture ponies without let-up, going for sensitive areas and discharges. Eyes can become inflamed. Use a repellant recommended by your vet.

Ponies with laminitis stand with their weight on the heels of the affected feet to relieve the discomfort in the most painful part – the toes.

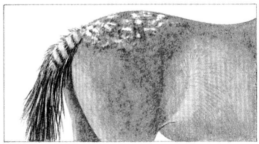

Insects attack open wounds so bring an injured pony in. Sweet itch is caused by midge bites at dawn and dusk, so stable the pony then or use a really good repellant.

Land management

Taking good care of your pony's field is most important.

Land must be well drained or it will be unusable in winter and never grow decent grass. If the land is yours or on a long lease, have a drainage system installed, if necessary. This is disruptive and expensive but well worthwhile.

Ditches should be kept clear of mud and weeds so water has a useful outlet. Ideally, ditches should be fenced off so ponies cannot fall into them and get stuck.

The bottom right picture shows a 'horse-sick' paddock. Ponies are fussy grazers. They reserve lavatory areas in their paddocks where they do their droppings, and will not normally graze there, so that grass is wasted. They eat other areas right down to the soil and also damage it with their hooves, especially in wet weather. The field soon looks uneven with some areas very cropped and others with long grass, weeds and droppings.

Land should be divided so you can use, treat and rest different parts in turn, so keeping the land healthy and able to grow decent grass.

If you want grass to form most of your pony's diet, you will need, on a year-round basis, about 1 hectare (2 acres) for one pony and 0.5 hectares (1 acre) for each additional pony, split into two or three paddocks.

LAYING DRAINAGE PIPES

DITCHING

HORSE-SICK FIELD

Each paddock must provide water and shelter. By placing your shelter shed centrally and using fences and gates to give or deny access to it, you can make one shed and trough serve three or more paddocks.

Ponies' droppings contain worm eggs, so to keep your land fairly clear of these harmful parasites you should pick up droppings every day, especially in warm, damp weather. Worming medicines (from your vet) are easily given from a plastic syringe placed in the corner of the mouth and squirted on to the back of the tongue.

Three important land treatments are harrowing, topping and fertilizing.

Harrowing roots out dead grass leaving room for new growth; **topping** cuts down the long grass in the 'loo' areas and elsewhere, encouraging new growth; and **fertilizing** feeds the soil so the grass can grow strong and healthy and provide good (but not over-rich) food.

Fertilizer firms can test your soil and advise on land care. If re-seeding is needed, tell the seed merchant you need a seed mix suitable for ponies and/or sheep. Rich dairy-cattle seed mixes are dangerous for ponies, who need poorish-quality grass as far as food content is concerned.

CLEARING DROPPINGS   WORMING

HARROWING

FERTILIZING

TOPPING

SHEEP CAN HELP KEEP PONY FIELDS LOW IN PARASITES

Feeding

It pays to look after your land as well-managed grass is cheaper food than hay and concentrates. If you sow a low-nutrient grass mix, or choose rented grazing carefully, there's no need for your pony to get fat.

But there are times when grass needs supplementing with hay and maybe concentrates (see volume 10: *Feeds and Feeding*). Hard-working ponies may need concentrates (but others rarely do), and in winter, when there's little goodness in grass, and mid-summer if the grass is eaten down or barely growing due to drought, you may need to feed hay to make up the lack of bulk and roughage (as well as food value) normally supplied by grass. If the grass is allowed to rest and grow, as well as being treated and fertilized, you'll find that you need relatively little supplementary feed, but if the field is overstocked (contains too many animals) and poorly managed, you may need to feed most of the year.

The old-fashioned idea of 'starvation paddocks' for laminitic ponies is wrong: lack of correct nutrients can actually encourage laminitis. Ask a vet or nutritionist (feed specialist, perhaps at the firm whose feeds you buy) about feeding such ponies.

All changes in feeding must be gradual, so don't feed your pony one day and not the next, or for only a couple of days before a weekend's work. This is quite wrong and can cause colic. Once you start feeding continue *every day*, decreasing amounts gradually over a week or more if you are going to stop because of changes in grass growth.

Try to feed concentrates, when used, twice daily (splitting the daily amount) as ponies' digestive systems work better this way.

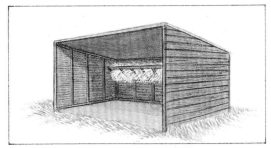

Feeding hay. A long wall rack in a shelter is ideal. Haynets should be tied at ponies' head height and to something firm so the pony can get the hay out easily.

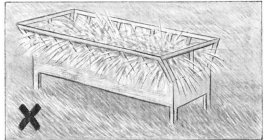

Feeding hay loose is wasteful: it blows away and gets trodden in mud. Cattle racks are not ideal for ponies, who may bump into them, causing injury.

Hay is best fed under cover, ideally where the ponies choose to shelter, and, like all feeds, there must be at least one more net than the number of ponies (unless in a long rack) so there's a spare pile for a timid one.

Space out concentrate containers well, about six paces apart, to discourage stealing and squabbling. Try to feed at the same times daily as ponies get used to this and their digestive systems work best that way. If you really can only feed once a day, feed at night.

The best food for keeping ponies warm in winter is a *constant* supply of hay, not concentrates. Concentrates give a quick boost of energy (for warmth) but this is soon over. Hay takes longer to eat and eating and digesting food creates heat, so hours spent eating hay create an inner 'central-heating system' for ponies!

If you stock up the field daily in winter with enough hay to last 24 hours, you'll really be helping the ponies.

Ponies with Arab and/or Thoroughbred blood will probably need concentrates in winter, even if not working. Ponies needing extra feeds should be brought out of the field so they can eat without harassment from others.

Feed the same ingredients in each feed as change can cause indigestion.

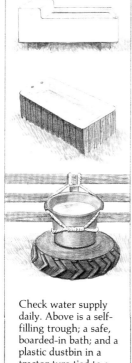

Check water supply daily. Above is a self-filling trough; a safe, boarded-in bath; and a plastic dustbin in a tractor tyre tied to a fence post.

Good field containers for concentrates are (from top): a travelling manger hooked to the fence; a wide cattle bucket (ponies dislike narrow containers); a bucket in a tyre for a pony who tips his bucket over; and a plastic washing-up bowl. Stay to supervise concentrate meal times: the 'field boss' here is being held to stop him stealing the others' feeds.

Remove containers after feeding.

Streams should be frequently checked for pollution, which can occur without warning due to agricultural pesticides, fertilizers and industrial poisons washing into them from the land or rivers.

Rugs and headcollars

A properly designed, well-fitting rug can be a big help to an outdoor pony in winter, particularly if he is of Arab or Thoroughbred blood or is clipped. If the rug is of bad design, a poor fit and, just as important, not properly maintained, it can do more harm than good and can actually seriously injure a pony.

Good rugs are 'pony-shaped': the back seam rises for the withers, dips for the back, rises again for the croup and dips at the tail. There are shaping darts at the stifles and, sometimes, at the elbows to take up slack material. They may also be tailored around the buttocks and neckline, all to produce a comfortable rug that stays in place using only breast straps and leg straps, or under-belly crossing surcingles.

Bad rugs are cut in a straight line down the back seam and have no proper shaping. They have a round-the-girth surcingle which is uncomfortable – and not only does it not keep the rug in place well but it actually holds it *out* of place when it shifts due to the pony rolling or moving about.

Good, modern rugs without this surcingle right themselves in action.

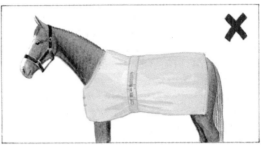

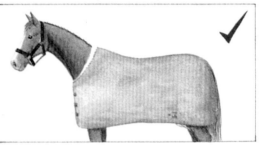

Poor, outdated style of rug (top) and too short to keep quarters warm. Good style (bottom) coming in *front* of the withers and right over the tail.

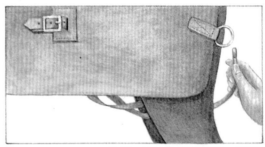

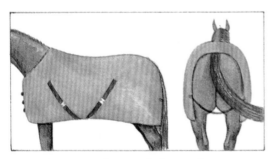

Crossing surcingles on a lightweight, comfortable, well-shaped synthetic rug, with fillet string to prevent the back blowing over the pony's head.

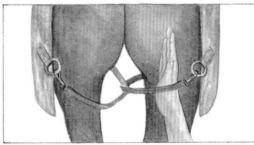

Hind leg straps link through each other before fastening. You should *just* be able to see them below a rug of normal depth, but not an extra-deep one.

You should just be able to fit the width of your hand inside leg straps or crossing surcingles. If tight, they restrict movement; if loose, the pony can get a leg caught when rolling or lying down.

Headcollars should not be left on ponies unless they are hard to catch, as the straps can get caught on branches etc. They are needed for catching, leading and tying up ponies.

You should easily be able to slide a finger all round under them and fit three fingers' width between noseband and face. If too large they can be rubbed off or could trap a hind hoof when the pony scratches his head; if too small they can irritate a pony and rub him sore, especially if left on.

Rugs and headcollars need frequent cleaning.

Leather headcollar with browband to stop headpiece slipping, three adjustment buckles and noseband mid-way between lips and sharp face bones. Correct fit.

Chrome leather 'field quality', but too small and tight, rubbing base of ears, face bones and jawbones. The pony could not move his jaws comfortably to eat.

Too-large **nylon headcollar**. Nylon is too strong to be left on in the field as it will not break if it gets caught, unlike leather, which is safer.

Spring clips – Spring (left) and trigger (right) clips correctly, and safely, fastened *away* from the head.

Double-length leadrope. If pony gets free and treads on one end it will pull through and fall away without bringing the pony down, like a clipped-on rope.

Tie a knot in the end of a **single rope** so if the pony pulls it will help prevent the rope being pulled through your hand and the pony getting free.

A short **catching strap** 50cm (6ins) long makes catching a difficult pony easier. A very short rope would do. The pony must not be able to tread on it.

Grooming and turn-out

Sometimes it is impossible to keep an outdoor pony looking presentable. In summer it's easy, but in winter, unless you have somewhere under cover, you can't keep the pony clean and dry.

Outdoor ponies need some natural oil in their coats for protection: a light body brushing in summer does no harm but a body brush won't be effective on a long winter coat. Don't try to brush off wet mud – you'll just push it in. Dandy it off when dry. Dry mud actually protects ponies from wind!

If there's a special event coming up, bring the pony into a well ventilated box the evening before to clean him up. If he's really filthy and wet hose him down thoroughly with clean lukewarm water, remove excess with a sweat scraper, rub him with straw or old towels and thatch him or put on a 'breathable' fabric rug. Dry his legs with towels, especially the heels, and bandage them. If the mud is dry, dandy it off or vacuum him. In summer he can dry off without clothing.

Unless the pony is exceptionally greasy, don't use shampoo – it can remove too much protective natural oil, and plain water will remove *some* oil anyway.

Don't clip more than necessary in winter: the pony really needs that hair! You can clip anywhere between the two extremes shown in the pictures. The more you clip, the more he'll need a rug, extra food and shelter.

Shorten the tail to hock level in autumn so it doesn't clog with mud or snow. It will regrow to help with flies in summer. The mane and forelock can be pulled to a medium length so you can plait up, yet still give some protection. If they are long, do a crest plait instead – quicker, easier and just as smart!

The breast-and-gullet clip (top) is ideal for an unrugged, native-type pony working in winter: the trace clipped pony (bottom) will need a rug, shed and extra feed.

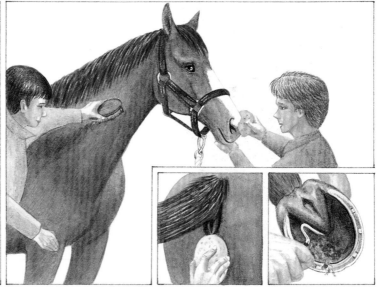

Daily grooming involves dandying off dry mud, picking out and checking feet and shoes, and damp sponging. In winter dry off after sponging with an old towel.

Shield the pony's eyes when using fly repellant If he's frightened of the hiss, stuff his ears with cotton wool or spray on to a rag then wipe the pony.

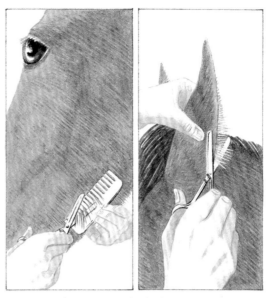

To trim the jaw, comb the hair up and snip it off through the comb teeth. Close the ears and carefully cut off hair which sticks out, never the hair inside.

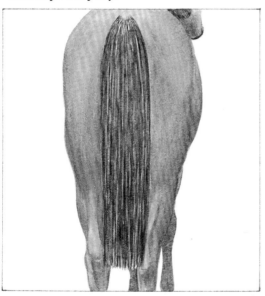

A racehorse tail, full at the top and banged at the bottom – ideal for outdoor ponies. Brush out mane and tail daily.

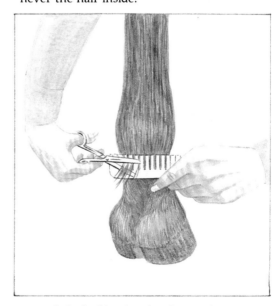

Trim fetlocks like this, but leave a little frond on the end (at the ergot) for drainage. A carefully trimmed outdoor pony can look quite smart.

Handling

Many outdoor ponies live in a herd situation and take their cues from each other as well as you. They gain confidence from their companions and may become over-familiar and pushy, or hare off in mock fright if one pony doesn't like being caught.

The thing is always to seem **calm** and **confident**, even if you aren't! If a herd of outdoor ponies senses that you are neither, they'll be on edge or may become bossy, and both are very difficult situations for a novice to handle.

It's easier to deal with your pony if you can separate him by bringing him in or by shutting yourselves in the field shelter, putting sliprails across its entrance. In bad weather, this is much better than being outdoors. A catching pen can also be used.

Never tie your pony up amongst others and leave him, as he may get bullied. Be confident and very firm with ponies who mill round, and push or smack them away on their necks or bellies.

If there is an aggressive pony, take an adult or experienced friend with you, but in established herds of friends you should have no problems.

You should catch your pony daily, examine him all over, groom him and treat any injuries, calling the vet, or other expert help if necessary. This keeps ponies disciplined. They soon become very independent of humans in a herd if not regularly handled.

Never rush or hassle ponies, especially if in a group. This annoys or upsets them and can make them difficult. The result could be an injury – possibly to you.

Approach a pony from the side, not from behind where he may not see you and be startled and kick out at your sudden appearance. Speak from a distance first.

If expecting resistance, put the rope over his neck so you've got hold of him while you put on the headcollar. It's easy to hold both, like this.

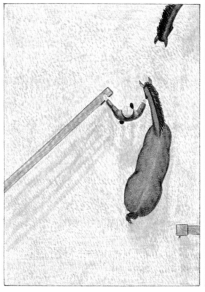

To cope with gate and pony, have the pony nearest the gatepost and open the gate just wide enough for safety. He'll help block other ponies' exit.

Fasten the gate! Lead into the field, turn the pony to face the gate and step back after letting go so you're out of reach of his heels if he whirls off.

Lead the pony through the first gate of a catching pen, fasten it, then lead through the next gate and fasten that. Pens are *very* useful, stopping escapes.

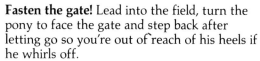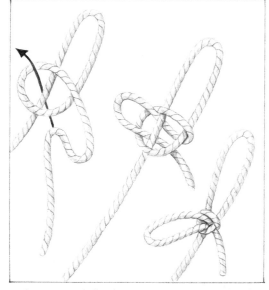

The Pony Club advise tying up a pony with a safety slip-knot (as shown), attached to a string loop which will break if the pony pulls back in fright. Binder twine is too strong.

Working and fitness

You may be surprised at how fit you can get your outdoor pony. Much depends on having poorish-quality grass so that you can feed almost as for a stabled pony, with concentrates for hard work. Grass should replace hay in spring and autumn (watch the pony's weight then) and maybe in summer. You should not be able to see your pony's ribs but *must* be able to feel them easily. Fat ponies cannot do hard work: it over-stresses them and can cause laminitis.

Your fitness programme is the same as for a stabled pony, but as outdoor ponies walk about a lot you can do less walking and more working trot in the early stages of your programme. Once two to four weeks of walking and trotting are achieved, proceed with faster work as normal.

If you keep his weight down and get him fit he can do almost any work you want at any time of year, and will be basically healthier than a confined stabled pony, and almost certainly happier. Remember, mental distress causes low physical well-being.

If you bring him in before a special event, he'll need his normal feed, hay and water, and a good bed in an airy box with windows, air vents and top door open.

Try to bring him home cool and dry. In summer you can turn him straight out to eat grass, feeding him later. In winter, he *must* be cool before going out, and dry if he's to wear a turn-out rug, otherwise he could get clammy under it and catch a chill. You may need to walk him around or dry him off in stable or shelter. Give hay first, then half a normal feed later and the rest last thing.

Do not give bran mashes: they are a sudden change from normal feeding, hard to digest and poorly balanced.

If a trace-clipped outdoor pony is given concentrates, turn-out rugs and a field shelter he can be as fit as a stabled pony and able to work hard.

Many endurance animals live almost entirely at grass but need to be super-fit. If they can do it so can your pony.

If you're going to be out with your pony all day, **do** let him graze when convenient (between classes, during a check out hunting) as long periods without food make him feel poorly, cause lack of energy and *can* cause indigestion and colic. You might be able to take a feed and/or hay in your box or car.

Also let him drink (up to half an hour before work) as lack of water, too, can cause indigestion, and dehydration in warm weather if the pony has sweated much. Endurance ponies must learn to drink en route during competitions to prevent this, and it's also useful for hunting ponies.

It is very wrong to deprive your pony of food and water for several hours before work as is often taught.

If chilly, walk the pony in a sheltered place and throw a rug or jacket over his loins and quarters at least.

A hairdryer can help but be careful of the flex. Use a circuit breaker.

Drying off a wet pony after work. If cold, walk the pony cool and dry him before putting on his rug and turning him out. Give him hay while you work.

A hard-working pony may need extra feed. Bring him out of the field so others do not steal it or harass him while he is eating.

The early walk/trot stage of a fitness programme is important and lays the foundation for gradually increasing faster work. Steady trot only when on roads!

Security

FREEZE-MARKED

R525

MICRO-CHIPPED

HOOF-BRANDED

FY5   2QQ

Outdoor ponies are more difficult to keep an eye on, so you must be security and thief conscious. **Do** get your pony freeze-marked, micro-chipped or hoof-branded for easy identification if stolen, and to deter thieves. They say that if thieves *really* mean to take your pony they will, but if you make things difficult for them they may feel he's not worth the bother and go elsewhere.

Try not to use isolated fields where thieves may not be noticed by locals. Try not to have gates opening on to public roads giving easy access for thieves. Ask locals to keep an eye out for lurking strangers; leave them your phone number. Thank those who help you with a gift at Christmas.

Keep gates strongly padlocked at both ends and use capped hinges, so the gate can't be lifted off. Have your hedges as high, thick and prickly as possible to deter thieves and keep other fencing strong and in good repair.

Have enough clear colour snapshots of your pony, and a written description with your name, address and phone number, to give to police, sales firms and local papers if he *is* stolen. Report his disappearance immediately.

Nearby neighbours may help spot thieves, but dwellings could house vandals!

Gates leading on to a private road may deter thieves.

This gate is firmly padlocked at both ends so even if thieves unscrew the hinges it's not an easy access.

The gate on the left on to the public road has been fastened shut and has a hedge growing across it so thieves cannot easily open it.

An aggressive pony can certainly discourage thieves if he hates strangers but can be a pest if he dislikes you too!

Public paths allow easy access for thieves and are a definite disadvantage in fields used for ponies.